ISMAILIS
A Celebration of Diversity

First published in 2010 by ISM Global Creations Inc., Canada
info@ismglobalphotos.com

Designed by Jessie Hall.

ISBN 978-0-9865314-0-8   Printed in China

ISMAILIS

A Celebration of Diversity

GOLD SPONSORS

Lalani Enterprises Ltd.
Victoria, BC

SILVER SPONSORS

BRONZE SPONSORS

INDIVIDUAL SPONSORS

Alykhan Sunderji	EconoLodge	Minaz Lalani	Tabreez, Maria and Zaydan Verjee
Ayaz Gulamhussein	Holiday Inn	Moez Moledina	The George Dawson Inn
Azeem & Shamira Asaria	Karim Somani & Family	Reena Lalji	
Daily Globe Newshop	Lens Save Express	Sarina Homes	
Dynamic Furniture Corp.	Lens & Shutter Cameras	Sadru Ladhani & Family	

Special thanks to all our sponsors
for their contributions and support.

PRESENTING SPONSORS

PREFACE

I love photography. It's a lifelong passion that grew as I travelled and wanted a way to preserve memories of the people and places I encountered. I love to inspire emotion from the images I take because a photograph suspends a moment in time, capturing a look, a feeling or a happening. I believe that photography is important to all cultures because it is a medium that allows individuals to express their relationships with the world without words. It is essential to the way we observe, communicate, remember, learn, share and most of all, celebrate.

Growing up in Calgary one of my greatest pleasures was bearing witness to the diversification of our community. Much of the early Canadian Ismaili Muslim community is from parts of Africa; many arrived here fleeing conflict and in search of new opportunities for their children. More than thirty years later the face of our population is different but the source of that diversity is familiar. In search of opportunities for their families, Ismaili Muslims have arrived from Afghanistan, Bangladesh, India, Pakistan, Tajikistan, Syria and beyond. We are bound together by our faith, but our cultural variations enrich us all.

For sometime now, I've been searching for a way to combine my passion for photography and my desire to give back to my community and to those less fortunate. About five years ago, as I was driving to work along the Bow River in Calgary (Alberta, Canada), I was awestruck by the beauty of the white, misty fog dancing above the river, and while in contemplation it came to me: "Wouldn't it be amazing to put together a book of photography about Ismailis from around the world, and donate the proceeds from the sale of the book to the Aga Khan Development Network." I knew there were many photography books showcasing cultures and countries, but I did not know of one that focused on Ismailis and celebrated our diversity. I immediately decided that this was something I wanted to create and share.

I am delighted to be able to share this book with you! It would not have been possible without the participation of the photographers who shared their work, and the generous contributions of our sponsors and volunteers.

Throughout this journey I received constant support and encouragement from my husband, Anish, my sister, Arzeen, my parents, Amir and Daulat, my parents in-law Pyarali and Laila, Aziz Uncle, my dear friends Reena and Ashifa, and Carmen Ryjulin and Aly Karmali from RBC. Thank you for believing in my vision.

As you flip through the pages I hope that you feel inspired by the moments in time captured by each of the photographs you see. I also hope that you, like me, will be in awe of the diversity and talent we have in the global Ismaili community.

Best wishes,

Ashifa Asaria-Lalani

GRAND PRIZE WINNER

HERstory
Badakshan, Tajikistan

Zahid Wissanji
Kampala, Uganda

WHAT INSPIRED YOU TO TAKE THE PHOTOGRAPH?

The woman is so beautiful. I was in Tajikistan, learning a little about the country and the history of its people, and there was this woman with the prints of time all over her face. She agreed to be photographed without hesitation, and from the look in her eyes, it seemed to me she wanted to be remembered.

WHAT DOES "DIVERSITY" MEAN TO YOU?

Diversity isn't just about a variety of ways, habits and thoughts. The word conjures an appreciation of that variety, beyond the simple recognition of difference, beyond tolerance, beyond judgment. And, since diversity amongst communities does not necessarily preclude unity under a common theme, it is something I cherish, because it is something that allows people to just be.

FIRST PLACE

Hanging Outside Jamatkhana
Hunza, Pakistan

Alim Boflo
Vancouver, Canada

WHAT INSPIRED YOU TO TAKE THE PHOTOGRAPH?

I was overwhelmed by the beauty of the location of the Jamatkhana. What a setting! Nestled in the mountains and valleys, it was breathtaking. I saw these kids enjoying themselves, just being kids, and I just had to capture that slice of life.

WHAT DOES "DIVERSITY" MEAN TO YOU?

Beauty. If you look through a kaleidoscope, you see many beautiful colours, patterns and shapes. Yet, there is symmetry, there are similarities when the image is presented as a whole. We come from many different parts of the world, but we are one giant family.

SECOND PLACE

Backyard Mandwo
Vancouver, Canada

Aliza Sovani
Manotick, Canada

WHAT INSPIRED YOU TO TAKE THE PHOTOGRAPH?

A little girl was the inspiration for the photograph. She was curious about
what I was doing and followed me as I took pictures. Watching her watch me,
I wondered what a photo taken by a child who was too little to carry a heavy
camera would look like. So I took this picture, to satisfy MY curiosity.

WHAT DOES "DIVERSITY" MEAN TO YOU?

In our Ismaili Muslim community, diversity means people of different
nationalities and cultures with the same ethics, values, and strong faith.

THIRD PLACE

Love
Mumbai, India

Nazim Lokhandwala
Mumbai, India

WHAT INSPIRED YOU TO TAKE THE PHOTOGRAPH?

The love that we have for our baby is very clear in this image. My wife tattooed my daughter's name on her back because she is very, very special to us. She was born to us after eight years of marriage.

WHAT DOES "DIVERSITY" MEAN TO YOU?

Diversity is the art of thinking independently, together.

Blossoming Friendship
Vancouver, Canada

Michelle Penny
Burnaby, Canada

Volunteer Tour Guides at Aleppo Citadel
Aleppo, Syria

Ayeleen Ajanee Saleh
Dhaka, Bangladesh

Citadel at Masyaf
Revitalization Project
Aga Khan Trust for Culture
Masyaf, Syria

Muslim Harji
Beaconsfield, Canada

Freedom
Cairo, Egypt

Farah Manji
Calgary, Canada

OPPOSITE PAGE

Life In the Mountains
Upper Hunza, Pakistan

Ali Ahmed
Islamabad, Pakistan

Life is not easy in the beautiful valleys of Northern Pakistan. The people are very hardworking. All family members, male and female work together to meet their day-to-day needs. You need to have the heart of a lion to cross this bridge.

A Fun Game Called Baba Baba
Kabul, Afghanistan

Khadija Alidad
Toronto, Canada

Nourishing the World, Nourishing Ourselves
Karachi, Pakistan

Raheel Lakhani
Karachi, Pakistan

Studying Together
Gulmit Gojal, Pakistan

Asghar Khan
Gilgit, Pakistan

An Ismaili Identity
Toronto, Canada

Haseena Manek
Toronto, Canada

I often wear this necklace. In it I see the diversity of Ismailis around the world. Like the multi-faceted quartz on the left, Ismailis are one unit with many faces. Our common religion is seen in the Allah pendant, while our cultural and geographic differences are apparent in the Africa pendant, representing my family's cultural heritage.

HONOURABLE MENTION

You and Your Faith, Nothing Else Matters
Berkeley, United States

Faheema Chaudhury
Northridge, United States

Market Seller
Shughnan, Afghanistan

Nabila Wissanji
Johannesburg, South Africa

Resting *Hunza, Pakistan* | Samina Khan *Calgary, Canada*

Warmth & Love *Hunza, Pakistan* | Safida Begum *Islamabad, Pakistan*

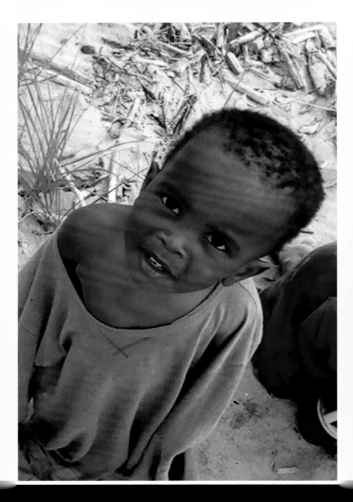

A New Ismaili *The Pinery Provincial Park, Canada*
Nalina Sacoor *Toronto, Canada*

mran Banele Kassam was born in South Africa and adopted by his

Afghans for Change *Toronto, Canada* | Aziz Dhamani *Toronto, Canada*

Variety occurs in form; in substance all is unified.

- *Rumi*

Man Made
Baluchistan, Pakistan

Amin Shallwani
Karachi, Pakistan

Monument of Convergence
Paris, France

Amin Ahmed
Sherwood Park, Canada

Bandra Jamatkhana Golden Jubilee Celebration
Mumbai, India

Nazim Lokhandwala
Mumbai, India

NEXT PAGE

Learning to Read
Chitral, Pakistan

Hashoo Foundation
Islamabad, Pakistan

Love for Knowledge
Gulmit Gojal, Pakistan

Noor Muhammad
Karachi, Pakistan

LEFT

These kids travel three miles, on foot, to attend
school every day.

Hopeful
Karachi, Pakistan

Raheel Lakhani
Karachi, Pakistan

My Desert Rose
Salamiya, Syria

Muslim Harji
Beaconsfield, Canada

OPPOSITE PAGE

Adorable Sisters
Victoria, Canada

Anish Lalani
Ottawa, Canada

Hangin' with Daddy
Calgary, Canada

Arzeen Kassam
Calgary, Canada

LEFT

HONOURABLE MENTION

Skywalk
Toronto, Canada

Rahim Bhimani
Toronto, Canada

On Our Way to the Canadian Ismaili Games
Vancouver, Canada

Zahed Lalani
Ottawa, Canada

Exploring the Delegation of the Ismaili Imamat
Ottawa, Canada

Rahim Bhimani
Toronto, Canada

Melbourne Central Station
Melbourne, Australia

Shaheryar Lakhani
Karachi, Pakistan

LEFT

Relaxing at Home
Mundra, India

Rozina Kanchwala
Saint Charles, United States

Beginning Life Together
Victoria, Canada

Ashifa Asaria-Lalani
Ottawa, Canada

LEFT

An Endless Smile
Dan-E-Zaminak, Afghanistan

Jehan Lalani
Calgary, Canada

A very warm-hearted Ismaili living in
the remote village of Dan-E-Zaminak,
Afghanistan amidst highly vulnerable,
mountainous terrain.

Her hair is coloured with henna and
she is wearing a traditional, hand-
embroidered Ishkashim. This hat is
given to elders in a village, recognizing
wisdom and signifying respect.

Her necklace is hand beaded, common
in this part of Central Asia.

Still Smiling in the Rain
Calgary, Canada

Fuad Sajwani
Calgary, Canada

Bridal Beauty
Calgary, Canada

Ashifa Asaria-Lalani
Ottawa, Canada
(Mendhi by Shafina Premji)

NEXT PAGE

Anticipating His Highness the Aga Khan's Arrival
Lisbon, Portugal

Shaleefa Juma
Saskatoon, Canada

After the Foundation Ceremony
Khorog Jamatkhana
Khorog, Tajikistan

Ayeleen Ajanee Saleh
Dhaka, Bangladesh

OPPOSITE PAGE

Volunteering at the Local Orphanage *Johannesburg, South Africa*
Nabila Wissanji *Johannesburg, South Africa*

Gulnar Carlisle Giving Back to Her Birth Country *Mombasa, Kenya*

Work No Words
Calgary Stampede Breakfast
Calgary, Canada

Mansur Shariff
Calgary, Canada

Ready to Serve
Johannesburg, South Africa

Nabila Wissanji
Johannesburg, South Africa

Our Women Volunteers
Gulmit Gojal, Pakistan

Ali Rehmat
Gilgit, Pakistan

Ready for the Rain
Vancouver, Canada

Iqbal Ishani
Vancouver, Canada

Mowla ke Shan
Salamieh, Syria

Ayeleen Ajanee Saleh
Dhaka, Bangladesh

59

Nature of Prayer
Ottawa, Canada

Nurin Merchant
Ottawa, Canada

This mixed media painting was a submission for "Colours of Love" organized by the Ismaili Council for Canada to commemorate the Golden Jubilee of His Highness the Aga Khan. The phrases Ya Allah, Ya Muhammad and Ya Ali are emerging from the tasbih. The colours: a hint of gold, bronze and blue, reflect nature at its best and the Golden Jubilee celebrations.

Awaiting His Highness the Aga Khan
Khorog, Tajikistan

Nabila Wissanji
Johannesburg, South Africa

Majestic Hunza Valley *Khorog, Tajikistan* | Ali Ahmed *Islamabad, Pakistan*

Harvest Time
Baghlan Province, Afghanistan

Jehan Lalani
Calgary, Canada

Day at the Beach
Toronto, Canada

Hamid Shamji
North York, Canada

Contemplation
Khorog, Tajikistan

Zahid Wissanji
Kampala, Uganda

65

Arches of the Ismaili Centre *Dubai, United Arab Emirates* | Hamid Jivraj *Mississauga, Canada*

Prayer Lights the Way
Vancouver, Canada

Asif Bhalesha
Delta, Canada

"What we celebrate today can be seen as a new creative link between the spiritual dimensions of Islam and the cultures of the West. Even more particularly, it represents another new bridge between the peoples of Islam and the peoples of Canada."
- *His Highness the Aga Khan, Inauguration of the Delegation of the Ismaili Imamat in Ottawa, Canada, December 6, 2008*

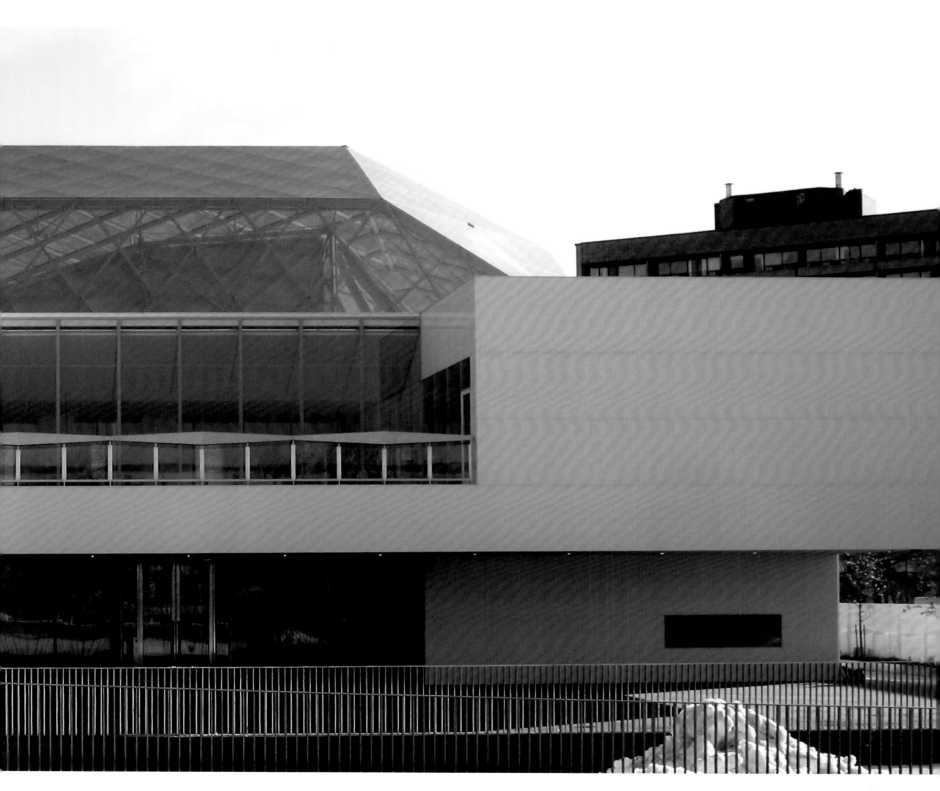

Delegation of the Ismaili Imamat *Ottawa, Canada* | Farhan Devji *Vancouver, Canada*

Light Through the Dome
Delegation of the Ismaili Imamat
Ottawa, Canada

Anish Lalani
Ottawa, Canada

Chalo re Sakhi Preetam ke Darbaar ("Friends, let us proceed to the Darbar of our Beloved" Hassanally G. Rammal)
London, England | Aly Sunderji *Burnaby, Canada*

Baking Cookies with Mommy *Ottawa, Canada* | Shafique Shamji *Ottawa, Canada*

Playing with Dad *Los Angeles, United States* | Mehboob Janmohamed *Calgary, Canada*

Daddy's Girl
Nairobi, Kenya

Arzina Bhanjee
Nairobi, Kenya

Beautiful Hanan
Salamieh, Syria

Asif Bhalesha
Delta, Canada

Adorned
Nairobi, Kenya

Moyez Charania
Sarasota, United States

Looking Out
Shughnan, Afghanistan

Nabila Wissanji
Johannesburg, South Africa

The Village of Baghi Payan
Afghanistan

Jehan Lalani
Calgary, Canada

LEFT

Rush
Grand Central Station
New York, United States

Fuad Sajwani
Calgary, Canada

Never Asleep
New York, United States

Fuad Sajwani
Calgary, Canada

Stillness, Ha' Penny Bridge *Dublin, Ireland* | Farah Bhanji *Toronto, Canada*

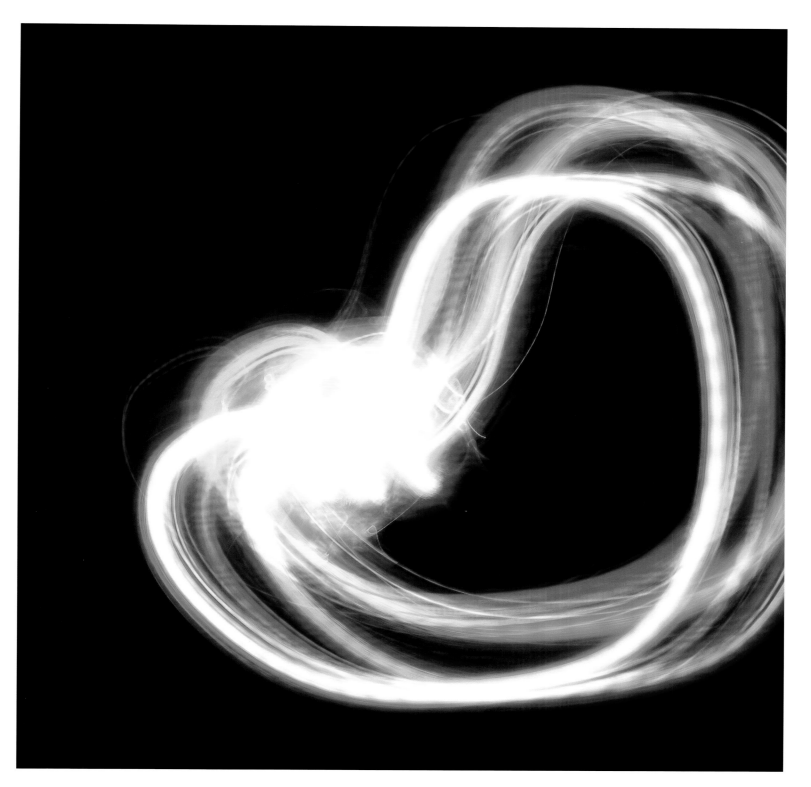

Painting Love with Light *Karachi, Pakistan* | Raheel Lakhani *Karachi, Pakistan*

All Dressed Up *Toronto, Canada*

Mother's Comfort
Vancouver, Canada

Ashifa Asaria-Lalani
Ottawa, Canada

Afghan Cultural Dance
Golden Jubilee Celebrations
Montreal, Canada

Muslim Harji
Beaconsfield, Canada

Safar Performance
Held during the
Golden Jubilee year.
Vancouver, Canada

Asif Bhalesha
Vancouver, Canada

OPPOSITE PAGE

Jubilation After Deedar
Ishkashim, Tajikistan

Ayeleen Ajanee Saleh
Dhaka, Bangladesh

Blocking the Sun *Khorog, Tajikistan* | Ayeleen Ajanee Saleh *Dhaka, Bangladesh*

Making Music
Las Vegas, United States

Shaleefa Juma
Saskatoon, Canada

In Harmony
Yasin Valley, Pakistan

Asghar Khan
Gilgit, Pakistan

USA Ismaili Band
Chicago, United States

Aziz Dhamani
Toronto, Canada

Watching Imamat Day Celebrations
Gulmit Gojal, Pakistan

Ali Rehmat
Gilgit, Pakistan

Ring of Fire
The Silk Route Festival
Gulmit Gojal, Pakistan

Asghar Khan
Gilgit, Pakistan

LEFT

Kampala Jamatkhana
Kampala, Uganda

Anish Lalani
Ottawa, Canada

Lit by the Moon
Tanga Jamatkhana
Tanga, Tanzania

Alkarim Pirmohamed
Dar es Salaam, Tanzania

OPPOSITE PAGE

Little Student
Chitral, Pakistan

Hashoo Foundation
Islamabad, Pakistan

Perseverance
Khorog, Tajikistan

Zahid Wissanji
Kampala, Uganda

Wisdom
Dushanbe, Tajikistan

Zahid Wissanji
Kampala, Uganda

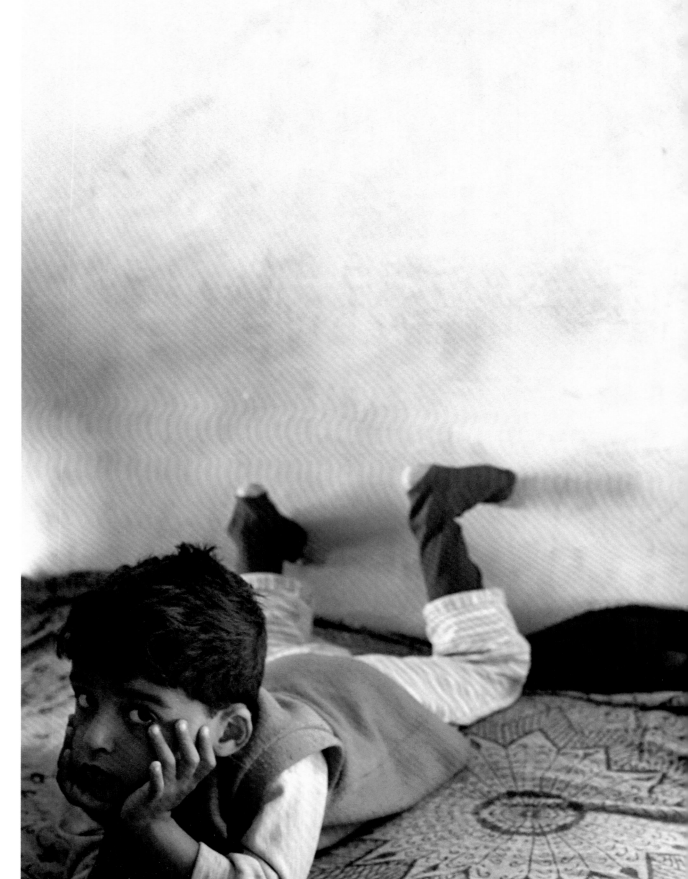

Nirdosh (Innocence)
Kutch, India

Rahim Pradhan
Toronto, Canada

Little Khizr *Karachi, Pakistan* | Amin Shallwani *Karachi, Pakistan*

Lions Gate Jamatkhana *North Vancouver, Canada* | Sultan Baloo *North Vancouver, Canada*

Gojal Jamatkhana
Gojal, Pakistan

Ali Rehmat
Gilgit, Pakistan

Gulmit Carpet Centre
Gulmit Gojal, Pakistan

Spice Bazaar
Aleppo, Syria

Nevin Harji
Beaconsfield, Canada

Roadside Fruit Vendor
Salamieh, Syria

Muslim Harji
Beaconsfield, Canada

**Mothers: Driving their
Children's Success**
Lira, Uganda

Salima Jaffer
Toronto, Canada

During an eight-month volunteer post in Kampala, Uganda with the Aga Khan Foundation Canada, I had the opportunity to travel to Northern Uganda with the Madrasa Resource Centre where I spoke with parents and teachers about the madrasas in their area. We visited poverty stricken, war torn Lira. There, mothers do it all: they feed their children (when food is available), clothe and bathe them, walk them to school, take them to the hospital when they are sick, do the farming, and help with homework.

I'm Little but I Can Make a Big Difference, World Partnership Walk *Ottawa, Canada*
Ashifa Asaria-Lalani *Ottawa, Canada*

World Partnership Walk Volunteers *Vancouver, Canada*
Iqbal Ishani *Vancouver, Canada*

We are people who need to Love,
because Love is the soul's life,

Love is simply creation's greatest joy.

- *Rumi*

Apart, yet Together
Masai Mara, Kenya

Ashifa Asaria-Lalani
Ottawa, Canada

Hiking the Kabul Wall
Kabul, Afghanistan

R. Chorshambiev
Coventry, England

Ismaili youth from eight countries (Afghanistan, Canada, France, India, Kenya, Pakistan, Tajikistan and USA) hike the Kabul Wall.

Zebras by the Tree
Ngorongoro, Tanzania

Azmina Karimi
Coquitlam, Canada

Blue
Mombasa, Kenya

Azmina Karimi
Coquitlam, Canada

Emerald Beauty *Lake Louise, Canada* | Aliza Sovani *Manotick, Canada*

Salim with a Prize-winning Salmon
Port Hardy, Canada

Gulnar Carlisle
North Vancouver, Canada

Water Wheel
Khorog, Tajikistan

Farah Bhanji
Toronto, Canada

The cans on this wheel collect water from the river. The water is poured
down a thin metal tray to the side of a pathway where local women gather
to wash their dishes.

Morning Mist *Al-Khawabi, Syria* | Derar Abbas *Tartous, Syria*

Livestock - A Key Source of Income
Hunza, Pakistan

Ali Ahmed
Islamabad, Pakistan

Peer Ali - A Student of Fine Arts
Karachi, Pakistan

Noor Muhammad
Karachi, Pakistan

Fall in the Fruit Orchard
Hunza, Pakistan

Ali Ahmed
Islamabad, Pakistan

Giggly, Silly, Funny
Khorog, Tajikistan

Zahid Wissanji
Kampala, Uganda

Birthday Wishes
Toronto, Canada

Azam Bhaloo
Toronto, Canada

OPPOSITE PAGE

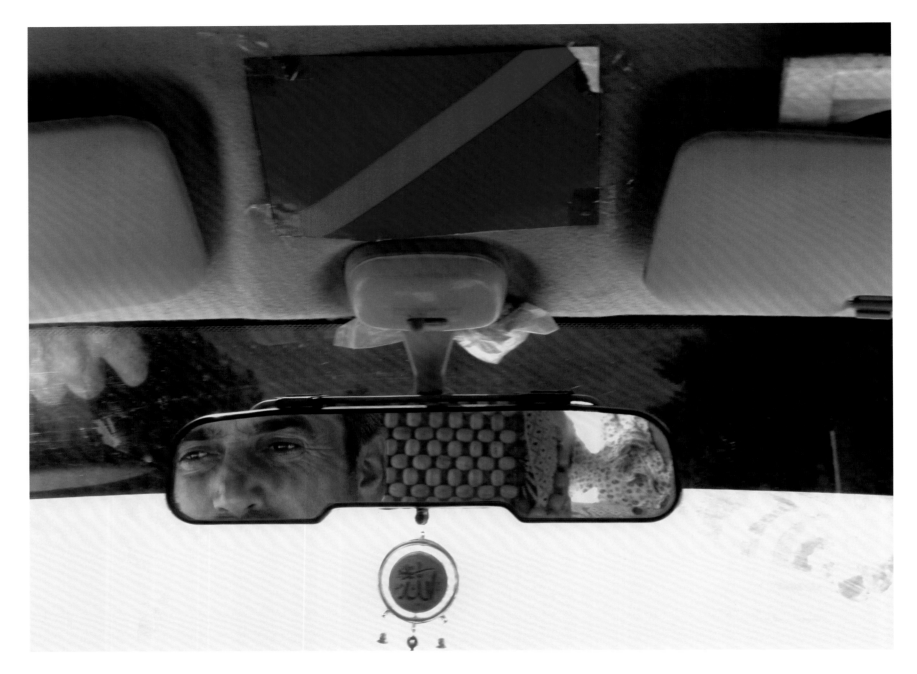

Taxi!!!
Khorog, Tajikistan

Alida Bata
Cheshire, England

During the Golden Jubilee Darbar, all taxis bearing the
Ismaili flag offered free rides.

Peeking Out
Pamir, Tajikistan

Sveta Juma
Khorog, Tajikistan

125

Golden Jubilee Arrival
Vancouver, Canada

Alamin Pirani
Coquitlam, Canada

Scout Troop - Ready for Inspection
Karachi, Pakistan

Nizar Noorali
Karachi, Pakistan

Golden Jubilee Celebrations *Toronto, Canada* | Aziz Dhamani *Toronto, Canada*

Steps of Inspiration
Gilgit, Pakistan

Deedar Ali
Gilgit, Pakistan

To celebrate the Golden Jubilee of His Highness Prince Karim Aga Khan the Ismaili Regional Council for Gilgit organized a three-day, 101 Km trek (September 6-8, 2007) on the Old Silk Route from Gilgit to Hunza. The goal was to recapture cherished memories of His Highness Prince Karim Aga Khan's first visit to the Northern area, and momentous stop in Hunza en-route, in 1960. His Highness's visit launched a new era of hope, prosperity and dignity in the lives of the community who had remained in seclusion for centuries.

After Darbar
Proshnev, Tajikistan

Ayeleen Ajanee Saleh
Dhaka, Bangladesh

Tasbih: A Constant Companion
North Vancouver, Canada

Sultan Baloo
North Vancouver, Canada

HONOURABLE MENTION
Snow & Souls
Ismaili Centre Burnaby
Burnaby, Canada

Aly Sunderji
Burnaby, Canada

OPPOSITE PAGE

Dani Traditional Dance, Silk Route Festival
Performed by Al Amyn Model School
Gulmit Gojal, Pakistan

Asghar Khan
Gilgit, Pakistan

India: Celebrating 50 Years of Freedom
Mumbai, India

Nazim Lokhandwala
Mumbai, India

Eager Student
Taldara, Syria

Ayeleen Ajanee Saleh
Dhaka, Bangladesh

The Violinist *Richmond Hill, Canada* | Fahrin Shariff *Richmond Hill, Canada*

Juicy Fruit *Richmond Hill, Canada* | Fahrin Shariff *Richmond Hill, Canada*

Fishing Boats
Mumbai, India

Nazim Lokhandwala
Mumbai, India

Umbrella on the Beach
Florida, United States

Nazim Suleman
Ajax, Canada

Swimming for the Gold
Canadian Ismaili Games
Vancouver, Canada

Asif Bhalesha
Delta, Canada

Jovial Nationalism
Golden Jubiliee Games
Nairobi, Kenya

Zahid Wissanji
Kampala, Uganda

LEFT

Endeavour
Minden, Canada

Rahim Bhimani
Toronto, Canada

Shaanti (Peaceful)
Burnaby, Canada

Aly Sunderji
Burnaby, Canada

ABOVE LEFT

Shannon Falls
Squamish, Canada

Asif Bhalesha
Delta, Canada

ABOVE RIGHT

A Monarch in my Garden
Vancouver, Canada

Gulnar Carlisle
North Vancouver, Canada

Ismaili Zizou in the Making
Scarborough, Canada

Alifa Somani
Scarborough, Canada

Hiding from his Brothers *Salamieh, Syria* | Farida Jivraj *Mississauga, Canada*

147

Elham
Qasimabad, Iran

Alim Boflo
Vancouver, Canada
ABOVE LEFT

Navid
Esfahan, Iran

Alim Boflo
Vancouver, Canada
ABOVE RIGHT

Blue-eyed Karim
Aleppo, Syria

Rozina Kanchwala
Saint Charles, United States

Always Looking Up!
Kandersteg, Switzerland

Alamin Pirani
Coquitlam, Canada

HONORABLE MENTION

Reflection
Kananaskis, Canada

Munira Jessa
Calgary, Canada

NEXT PAGE

Canadian Pride
Calgary, Canada

Shaleefa Juma
Saskatoon, Canada

Harbour View
Vancouver, Canada

Nazim Suleman
Ajax, Canada

ABOVE

Water Taxi
Victoria, Canada

Anish Lalani
Ottawa, Canada

Roadside Rhubarb
Badakshan, Tajikistan

Matoke (Plantains)
Kabale, Uganda

Anish Lalani
Ottawa, Canada

Santosh (Contentment)
ABOVE

Shukur (Thank You)
OPPOSITE PAGE

Kutch, India

Rahim Pradhan
Toronto, Canada

Bangles *India* | Salina Kassam *Toronto, Canada*

Homemade Naan for Sale *Kabul, Afghanistan* | Khadija Alidad *Toronto, Canada*

A Way of Life *India* | Salina Kassam *Toronto, Canada*

Baltit Fort
Hunza, Pakistan

Ali Ahmed
Islamabad, Pakistan

More than 700 years old, the Baltit
Fort is perched on the terraced slopes
of Karimabad surrounded by a majestic
mountain range. The Fort was the first
major intervention by the Aga Khan
Historic Cities Program, completed in
1996. The Fort is a cultural centre and
museum of local history.

Laundry Day
Bamyan, Afghanistan

Khadija Alidad
Toronto, Canada

Winter Sisters
Banff, Canada

Fuad Sajwani
Calgary, Canada

Winterland
Ottawa, Canada

Farzana Jiwani
Ottawa, Canada

The Warmth of their Smiles
Ishkashim, Tajikistan

Amirali Virani
Buffalo Grove, United States

Little Miss Sunshine
Nairobi, Kenya

Sameera Nanji
Nairobi, Kenya

ABOVE LEFT

My Flag Boy
Toronto, Canada

Zeenat Habib
Naperville, United States

ABOVE RIGHT

Just Cute!
Khorog, Tajikistan

Nabila Wissanji
Johannesburg, South Africa

Four Generations
Vancouver, Canada

Ashif Jumani
North Vancouver, Canada

Three Generations Enjoying a Stroll *Tashkurgan, China* | Alim Boflo *Vancouver, Canada*

There is only One Light,

and "you" and "me" are holes in the lampshade.

- Mahmud Shabistari

Friendship
Shugnan, Afghanistan

Nabila Wissanji
Johannesburg, South Africa

Cultural Beauty
Toronto, Canada

Imran Jamal
Thornhill, Canada

OPPOSITE PAGE

Beautiful Wisdom
Proshnev, Tajikistan

Ayeleen Ajanee Saleh
Dhaka, Bangladesh

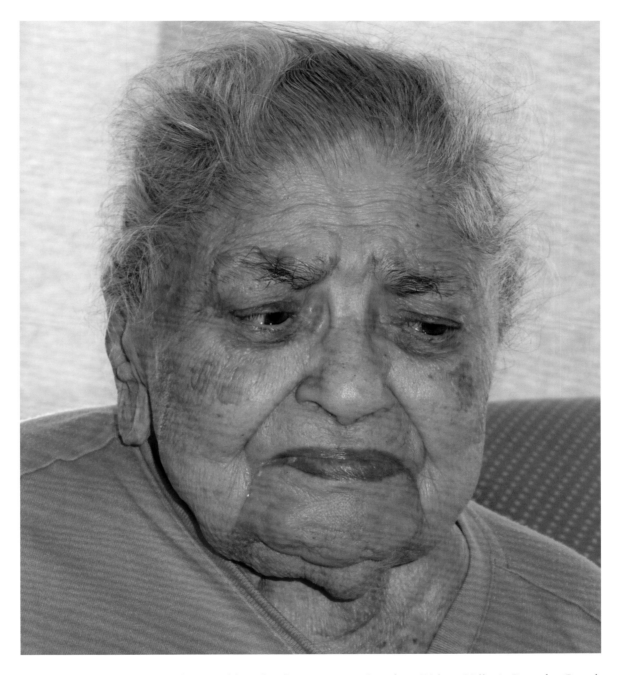

The Wrinkles of Life *Vancouver, Canada* | Rishma Vallani *Burnaby, Canada*

My grandmother, 97 years of age: born in India, married in Africa, passed away in Canada.

Carrying Water Home
Kabul, Afghanistan

Khadija Alidad
Toronto, Canada

A New Family Home
Pul-e-Khumri, Afghanistan

Diamond Kanji
Calgary, Canada

**En Route from Dushanbe
to Khorog**
Gorno Badakhshan, Tajikistan

Amirali Virani
Buffalo Grove, United States

Majestic
Khorog, Tajikistan

Zahid Wissanji
Kampala, Uganda

Hiking in Yoho National Park
British Columbia, Canada

Shehnaz Nurmohamed
Calgary, Canada

OPPOSITE PAGE

Freshly Washed
Khorog, Tajikistan

Nabila Wissanji
Johannesburg, South Africa

The Observer
Khorog, Tajikistan

Zahid Wissanji
Kampala, Uganda

ABOVE

Rooftop Ismaili Flag
Al-Khawabi, Syria

Farida Jivraj
Mississauga, Canada

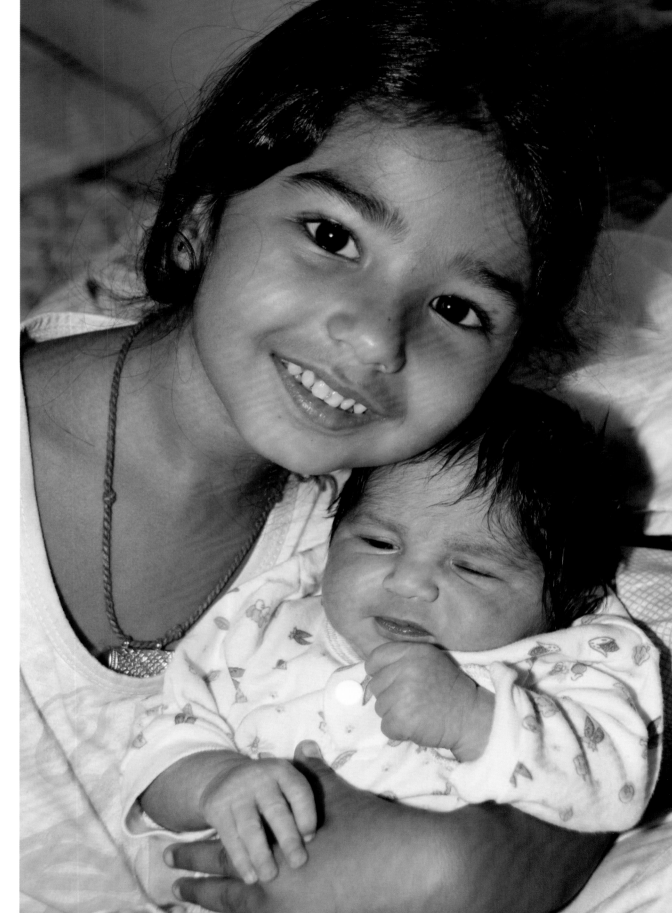

Sibling Love
Dar es Salaam, Tanzania

Alkarim Pirmohamed
Dar es Salaam, Tanzania

Bath Time! *Bamyan, Afghanistan* | Khadija Alidad *Toronto, Canada*

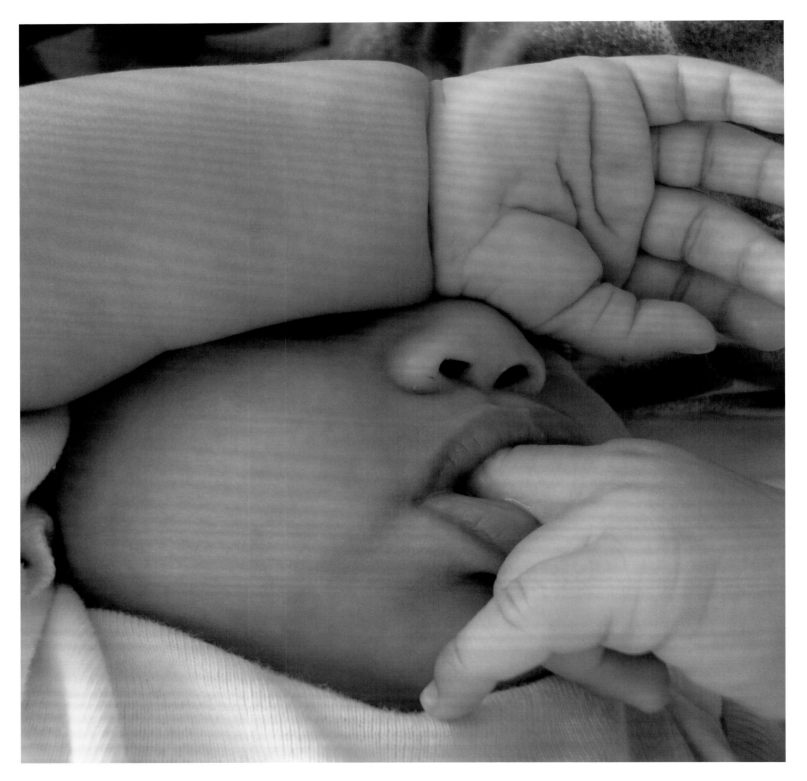

Princess Ilyana's had a Long Day!   *Ottawa, Canada* | Zahed Lalani *Ottawa, Canada*

Togetherness
Lisbon, Portugal

Nalina Sacoor
Toronto, Canada

Stampede Parade
Calgary, Canada

Shaleefa Juma
Saskatoon, Canada

Agricultural Festival of Seed Bowing *Gulmit Gojal, Pakistan* | Asghar Khan *Gilgit, Pakistan*

Homes Around the Altit Fort
Hunza, Pakistan

Afiz Jiwa
Coquitlam, Canada

Ismailis Living in Hasanabad
Mumbai, India

Jehan Lalani
Calgary, Canada

OPPOSITE PAGE

Beautiful Angel
Khorog, Tajikistan

Natasha Walji
Toronto, Canada

Empowering Women through Honey Bee Farming *Gilgit, Pakistan*
Hashoo Foundation *Islamabad, Pakistan*

Mode of Transportation *Sheberghan, Afghansitan* | Khadija Alidad *Toronto, Canada*

197

Donkey Carriage
Badakshan, Tajikistan

Zahid Wissanji
Kampala, Uganda

Shepherd
Tartous, Syria

Hamid Jivraj
Mississauga, Canada

Connections *Cabo Delgado, Mozambique*
Noreia Sacoor *Toronto, Canada*

Exhilaration
Murchison Falls, Uganda

Ashifa Asaria-Lalani
Ottawa, Canada

Expecting
Samburu Game Reserve, Kenya

Asif Bhalesha
Delta, Canada

HONOURABLE MENTION

Close to my Heart
Houston, United States

Sharmyn Ali
Sugarland, United States

Life is full of colour but there are lessons to be learned from the experiences that one goes through. This painting illustrates that life may not be easy to live, but hope and faith in God can make it simple.

Chippy *Gatineau Park, Canada* | Nazmu Mamdani *Ottawa, Canada*

Concrete Jungle Meets Serene Green *Hong Kong SAR, China* | Farhan Daya *Calgary, Canada*

Downtown
Nairobi, Kenya

Ashifa Asaria-Lalani
Ottawa, Canada

Love,

the supreme Musician,

is always playing in our souls.

- Rumi

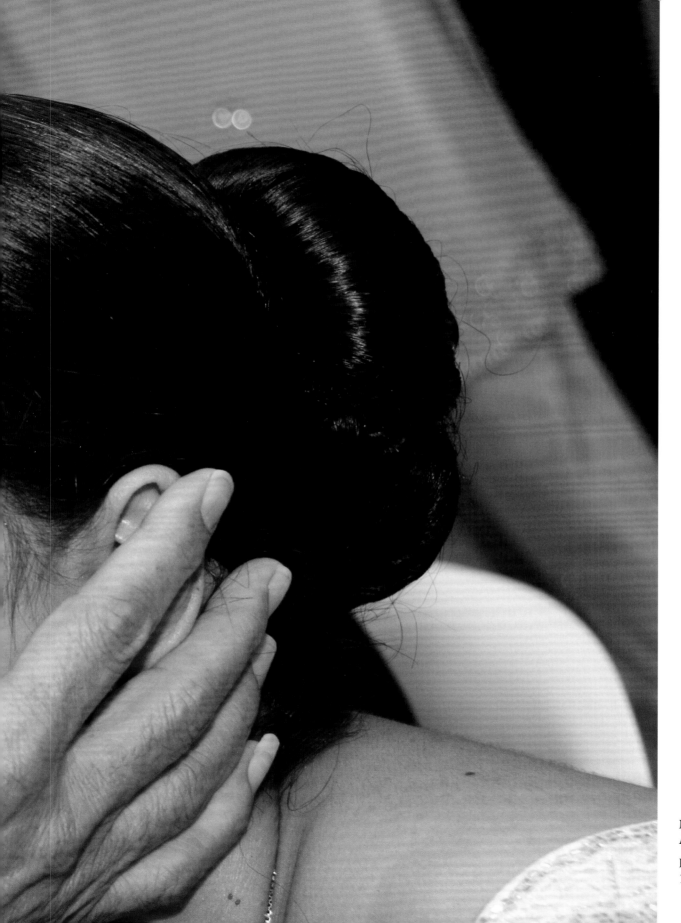

My New Daughter
Los Angeles, United States

Rahim Pradhan
Toronto, Canada

Young Pamiri Bride
Pamir, Tajikistan

Sveta Juma
Khorog, Tajikistan

The traditional wedding dress and national
beads worn by this young bride are passed
down from one generation to the next.

Intricate Design
Calgary, Canada

Shafeena Premji
Calgary, Canada

White Sari Bride
Calgary, Canada

Ashifa Asaria-Lalani
Ottawa, Canada

Aleppo Citadel Lookout *Aleppo, Syria* | Farida Jivraj *Mississauga, Canada*

Paradise
Kota Bharu, Malaysia

Farhan Daya
Calgary, Canada

Golden Light
Muskoka, Canada

Azam Bhaloo
Toronto, Canada

Friendship Beyond Boundaries
Baghlan Province, Afghansitan

Jehan Lalani
Calgary, Canada

The man on the left is an Ismaili shepherd who wanders the Gul Dara valley while the man on the right is a driver for FOCUS Afghanistan. These men lead very different lives, but their friendship persists despite the rural-urban divide.

Old Friends: Watching Festivities at Ruz e Noor
Khorog, Tajikistan

Nabila Wissanji
Johannesburg, South Africa

Laughter & Joy
Dallas, United States

Aziz Dhamani
Toronto, Canada

A Sweet Bite *Kampala, Uganda* | Ashifa Asaria-Lalani *Ottawa, Canada*

Welcome to TK!
Dushanbe, Tajikistan

Zahid Wissanji
Kampala, Uganda

Solace
Cape Town, South Africa

Arzeen Kassam
Calgary, Canada

The Pride of Aswan
Mausoleum of Sultan Muhammad
Shah, Aga Khan III
Aswan, Egypt

Hanan Al-Maghout
Damascus, Syria

OPPOSITE PAGE

… diversity itself is a gift of the Divine, and…embracing diversity

is a way to learn and to grow -
not to dilute our identities
but to enrich our self-knowledge.

*- Excerpt from "The Peterson Lecture" by His Highness the Aga Khan
to the Annual Meeting of the International Baccalaureate,
Atlanta, Georgia, USA, April 18, 2008*

APPENDIX

PAGE 31

Variety occurs in form; in substance all is unified.
- Rumi

CLOCKWISE FROM TOP LEFT

1

Our Young Volunteers
Montreal, Canada

Muslim Harji
Beaconsfield, Canada

2

In the Garden
Karachi, Pakistan

Mavia Siddiqui
Karachi, Pakistan

3

**Volunteering at the
World Partnership Walk**
Ottawa, Canada

Ashifa Asaria-Lalani
Ottawa, Canada

4

Senior Member
Tashkurgan, China

Asghar Khan
Gilgit, Pakistan

5

Family
Hunza, Pakistan

Samina Khan
Calgary, Canada

6

**From Tajikistan and
Living in China**
Tashkurgan, China

Alim Boflo
Vancouver, Canada

7

**Dedicated Volunteer:
World Partnership Walk**
Ottawa, Canada

Ashifa Asaria-Lalani
Ottawa, Canada

8

Amara, Learning to Walk
Hong Kong SAR, China

Leila Borrows
Hong Kong SAR, China

PAGE III

*We are people who need to Love, because Love is the soul's life,
Love is simply creation's greatest joy.*
- Hafiz

CLOCKWISE FROM TOP LEFT

1

Learning to Plant
Karachi, Pakistan

Raheel Lakhani
Karachi, Pakistan

2

My Hat
Hunza, Pakistan

Samina Khan
Calgary, Canada

3

Our Class
Sindh, Pakistan

Ashraf Devshi
Karachi, Pakistan

4

A Lifetime of Dedication
Kabul, Afghanistan

Masooda Shahi
Richmond, Canada

5

Curious
Ishkashim, Afghanistan

Alida Bata
Cheshire, England

6

**My Happiness Lies
in a Child's Smile**
Cairo, Egypt

Hanan Al-Maghout
Damascus, Syria

7

Empowering Through Education
Chitral, Pakistan

Hashoo Foundation
Islamabad, Pakistan

8

**Strength Through Our Volunteers,
World Partnership Walk**
Toronto, Canada

Aziz Dhamani
Toronto, Canada

9

13th Burnaby Ismaili Venturers
Kanderjam, Switzerland

Alamin Pirani
Coquitlam, Canada

PAGE 171

There is only One Light,
and "you" and "me" are holes in the lampshade.
- Mahmud Shabistari

CLOCKWISE FROM TOP LEFT

1
Volunteering at the
World Partnership Walk
Ottawa, Canada

Anish Lalani
Ottawa, Canada

2
Ismaili Youth
Karachi, Pakistan

Shaheryar Lahani
Karachi, Pakistan

3
Pumpkin Pie
Markham, Canada

Hamid Shamji
North York, Canada

4
Celebrating Our Birthdays
Ottawa, Canada

Salima Shamji
Ottawa, Canada

5
Marching on Imamat Day
Hunza, Pakistan

Ali Rehmat
Gilgit, Pakistan

6
Mother, Daughter & Niece
Vancouver, Canada

Moyez Charania
Sarasota, United States

7
A Beautiful Smile
Al-Khawabi, Syria

Ayeleen Ajanee Saleh
Dhaka, Bangladesh

8
Spending Time with
Our Grandmother
Gilgit, Pakistan

Samina Khan
Calgary, Canada

9
A Journey
Marrakesh, Morocco

Zehmina Kassam
Calgary, Canada

PAGE 209

Love, the supreme Musician, is always playing in our souls.
- Rumi

CLOCKWISE FROM TOP LEFT

1
My Late Grandfather who
Loved to Watch Hockey
Mississauga, Canada

Husseinali Hussein
Mississauga, Canada

2
A Hug from My Sister
Paris, France

Farzana Thawar
Toronto, Canada

3
Together
Gilgit, Pakistan

Sultan Ahmed
Gilgit, Pakistan

4
Dancing at Kushiali
Celebrations
Vancouver, Canada

Ashif Jumani
Vancouver, Canada

5
Soaking in the Sky
Toronto, Canada

Najda Kassam
Toronto, Canada

6
Mendhi Night
Ottawa, Canada

Safiq Devji
Ottawa, Canada

7
Warmth & Love
Toronto, Canada

Rahim Bhimani
Toronto, Canada

8
Volunteering in the Rain
Vancouver, Canada

Iqbal Ishani
Vancouver, Canada

9
Sharing a Hug
Calgary, Canada

Geeta Alizada
Calgary, Canada

10
Friends
Tashkurgan, China

Alim Boflo
Vancouver, Canada

SPONSOR ADVERTISEMENTS

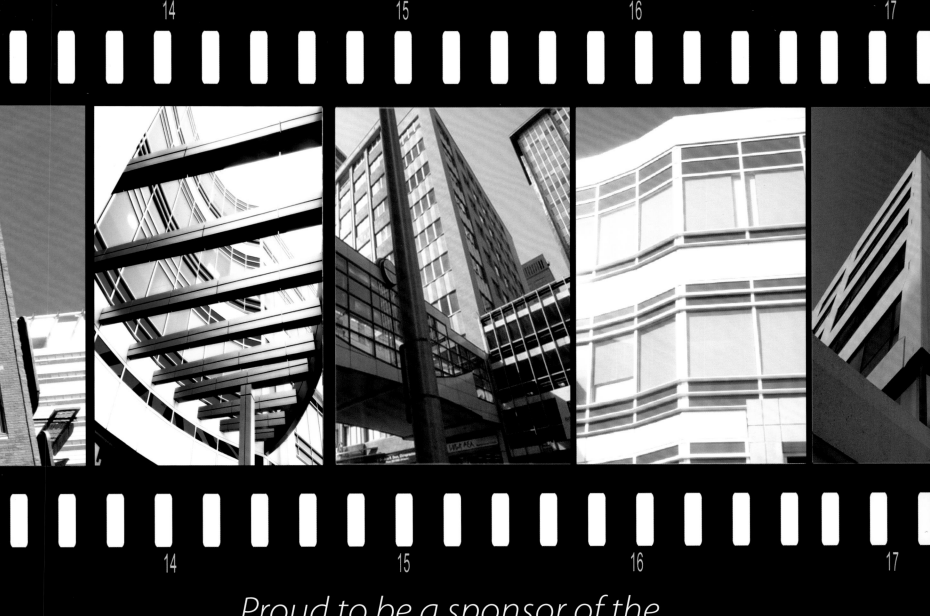

Proud to be a sponsor of the
International Ismaili Photography Competition.
Congratulations to the Winners!

*"Creating value others can't
by seeing what others don't."*

STRATEGIC

creative | design | branding

THANK YOU

I would like to express my deepest thanks for the opportunity to design this book and be a part of the project.

Learning about the Ismaili culture has truly been an uplifting experience. The appreciation that the Ismaili community has for its diversity is an inspiration to all.

Congratulations to all of the photographers who so beautifully captured the Ismaili community world-wide.

www.jessiehall.com

online design & development

new media consulting, social media,

online presence, search engine optimization,

graphic design, photography

we'll do the thinking for you.

thought bubble studios

info@thoughtbubble.ca   www.thoughtbubble.ca

LIFE WITHOUT THE ARTS.

RBC supports artistic endeavours in Canada,
because life without the arts would leave us all in the dark.

We are proud to support the
International Ismaili Photography competition.

Every photo tells a story.

A story of hope built on a unique Canadian partnership between Aga Khan Foundation Canada and organizations such as RBC in some of the most isolated and impoverished regions of the world.

Learn more by visiting akfc.ca.

RBC

AGA KHAN FOUNDATION CANADA

Sincere thanks for your support, input and advice:

Alnashir Asaria

Alnoor Devji

Aly Karmali

Amir & Daulat Asaria

Anish Lalani

Arif & Naila Lalani & Family

Arzeen & Imtiyaz & Family

Ashifa Jiwani

Aziz Bhaloo & Family

Ayaz Gulamhussein

Carmen Ryjulin

David Reyes

Farah Sunderji

Farhan Daya

Farzana Jiwani

Huma Pabani

Ismaili Mail

Jessie Hall

Malik Merchant

Moe Somani

Najib Jamal

Nazir Sunderji

Pyarali & Laila Lalani & Family

Reena Lalji

Saleema Sunderji & Family

Shakeel Hirji

Shellina Lakhdir

Tara Fleming